Trouble in an empty room

A Writing Collection from N. Sandwell

Introduction

I have always had a very vivid imagination. Maybe it is something to do with being an only child and having to entertain myself. My problem is that this imagination can become a bit too real at times. I can imagine and overthink scenarios until they become almost a reality. They can actually have a physical effect on me. I'm the same whilst reading. I don't think I always react in a normal way. Thrillers make my heart beat a bit too fast.

During my working life, I had constant distractions. The safety of others depended on my concentration. When I found myself unable to work and without these distractions, my imagination went wild. Different stories, conversations and scenarios taking root in my head. I want to write because I enjoy it. I need to write to get it out of my head!

So, I am aware that this is a strange mix of fun, sad and, at times, rude. My lovely wife would also say that there is some "arty farty crap" in here too.

I hope that amongst the poems, short stories and monologues, there is something for you to enjoy.

Thank you:

- to my Lovely Ness – a true beta reader. I love you.

- to Henry, my biggest cheerleader, "God only sent me one, but he sent me a good one."

- to my lovely Mum and Dad, always there for me, and I didn't give you a moment's worry until I was 51!

- to my 'younger than me' friend Shari for encouraging me to write.

- to Kath the most inspiring teacher – ever.

- to Linda who gave me back my voice.

- to Sylvia, the life enhancer.

Trouble in an Empty Room

It's often said that I could cause

Trouble in an empty room.

I don't seek out this disorder.

But around me, problems bloom.

I just want to mind my business

Avoiding stresses that loom.

But weird things seem to surround me,

See me coming, I presume.

I head towards any mischief.

My fate directed by whom?

At times like being in a play

With no lines, script or costume.

No point trying to avoid it

I'll hurtle toward my doom,

Embrace chaos and disarray

Time for peace when I'm in my tomb.

In heaven, God will greet me with

"Mr Mischief, I presume?"

The Paper Shop

The paper shop is opposite my house. I can see it from the front room window. I watch the people going in and out. They have sweeties in there. I like sweeties.

An old man and an old lady own the shop. They are about 50 or a hundred, I think.

Mummy takes me in there when we get off the bus. The sweeties are in front of the counter. The ones in tubes and packets, anyway. The wall behind the counter is all sweetie jars and dirty cigarettes.

The fancy boxes of chocolates are around the top. I have to bend my neck back to see them. We don't buy them, though, as my Aunty Mary gets our chocolates from the shop she works in. I like the Weekend Selection best.

I like chocolate cigarettes. You can eat the paper too. You can't eat any other type of paper. I've tried and grown-ups don't like it. They really don't like it if it is your school reading book.

The comics and magazines are on the other wall—the magazines on the pole I'm not allowed to look at. Mummy makes me look away. Sometimes she puts her hands over my eyes. I think it's because she doesn't want me to feel sad for the ladies in the magazines. I think they must be very poor because they can't afford clothes. They seem happy because they are always smiling. Mummy says the paper shop man is VERY naughty because he should put them up high.

I don't think that he is naughty, though, as he always says please and thank you.

Mummy says good boys always say please and thank you. I'm a good boy, so I get sweeties.

The Dating Game

So, I met this man

He's older than me.

I'm really keen and

I think he'd agree.

I've met all his friends.

Their wives are older.

They seemed very nice,

So, no cold shoulder.

They talked about things,

I don't understand.

Portfolios, shares

And stuff that expands.

I'll admit that it

Went over my head.

I played with their dog,

A Shih Tzu called Fred.

The hostess had done.

A really nice spread

Posh and organic,

With artisan bread.

No chicken nuggets!

Polenta with kale.

So posh, even the

Picnic eggs – quail!

So, sausage on sticks,

I just couldn't see.

Beef carpaccio

Just wasn't for me.

So, on the way home,

Had my favoured dish,

Stopped at McDonald's

For Filet of Fish.

Well, he didn't mind,

Thought he'd stay over.

Packed a bag, I said;

"Cool your jets, Rover.

Just because I'm keen,

Don't mean I'm easy,

Besides those quail eggs

Have made me queasy.

Text me tomorrow.

No use debating."

Won't do any harm,

To keep him waiting.

So, next, he decides.

That we'll go away.

Hotel with a spa

For a three-night stay.

Come Friday, we go,

I'm so excited.

I see the hotel,

I'm just delighted.

Just imagine me

In a five-star joint.

Travel Lodge only

Up until this point.

Well, I'm wined and dined,

We stay in a suite.

It's got a doorbell!

The perfect retreat.

Well, the time has come,

Now there's some passion.

He's pleased my dress is

Easy unfasten.

But then he spoils it,

Says, "Call me daddy."

Put my dress back on

And called a cabby.

But before I went

I just told him straight.

"You might be charming,

Rich and handsome, mate.

I've got one Daddy,

He's more than enough.

I wanted true love,

Not this kinky stuff.

So, what would be next,

Blindfolds and thigh boots?

Light bondage and whips

And all those pursuits?

I thought you liked me,

I was sure you did.

But you must have thought,

I'm a stupid kid.

I may not be bright

and I know that's true,

But I'm too clever

To be fooled by you.

You can keep your charm.

And shove your money.

I value myself,

I'm not your Honey.

My Dad would go mad,

If he only knew.

He'd knock your block off.

He's younger than you!"

With that, I escaped.

A cab was waiting.

With my pride intact

And no more dating.

Fell for the driver.

He's really a dish.

Guess what's his favourite?

A Filet of Fish.

My Nan's Flood

The 11th November 1977 was a particularly windy day. I almost got blown away on the way to school. I often stayed with my Nan at her bungalow, but I had a swimming lesson that night and it was also my 8th birthday, so I stayed at home. My Nan went to take her neighbour's dog for a walk and soon came back as the weather was so wild at the top of Chatsworth Avenue. She went to bed to read one of her favourite large print romances. The next thing that she noticed was that her bed was floating. It was obviously a good chapter.

She was only a little woman and the water came past her middle. Her neighbour from next door joined her and they soon took up residence in my Nan's kitchen. The neighbour perched on the draining board. She was quite a large lady and my Nan often used to complain that that the draining board never recovered and that after the flood things always rolled into the sink! At some point they decided to make some Horlicks – not thinking that the flooded fridge contained more sea water than milk. At some point someone shouted that they must turn out the light, as it was obviously too dangerous to use the electricity. My Nan replied, "If I'm going to drown – I'm not going to do it in the dark!" (There may have been a swear word included in this statement – but she was under stress). They were eventually rescued by a Sea Cadet boat and sailed down Chatsworth Avenue. When she arrived at the West View roundabout she was bundled into the back of an ambulance. She started protesting that her son lived in a bungalow on the other side of the roundabout. Thinking she was in shock and insistent that she needed to be checked in hospital they ignored her. My Nan was made of sterner stuff and she burst out of the back of the ambulance and ran barefoot across the roundabout to our house. (The flood incidentally stopped at our gates).

My Mum and Dad were woken by a hammering on the door. My Dad looked out of the window and then returned to bed. "Bill, who was it?" asked my Mum. "Oh, it was just my Mam wrapped in an eiderdown," he replied. He now says it was only as he said it out

loud that he processed what he'd seen.

I was woken up by a very cold Nan joining me in my bedroom, smelling of one or three medicinal brandies. I asked her what was going on and she simply said, "I've sailed down Chatsworth Avenue in a Sea Cadet boat." It seemed perfectly reasonable to the newly eight- year-old me and I went straight back to sleep.

The following day, I was disappointed to have missed all the fun. I was allowed to go the bottom of

Chatsworth Avenue to watch my Dad and Uncle Jimmy bravely wade up to the bungalow to rescue Joey the budgie!

My Nan had no house insurance, but Fleetwood pulled together and local charities did so much to help. Her carpets were collected and dried out by the ICI. However, her settee could always produce salt if you banged the arms hard enough.

Ocean

A sailor wants the sky and surf

Needing much more than stone and turf.

Floating along the mighty deep,

Sharing the brine of Neptune's keep.

Whales dance and the mermaids sing

Spume flies amidst salt-water sting.

Living a life formed by the tide,

To plunge the depths of life's big ride.

And when life ends with one last kiss,

I'll rest in this floating abyss.

I find it a touching notion,

To be eternally ocean.

In confidence alone

It was a lovely idea, the piano in the precinct. It just sat there waiting to be played, painted in bright colours, swirling up the sides and over the lid. People of all ages wandered up to play, from little children banging out 'Twinkle, Twinkle, Little Star' to older people playing the tunes of their youth. Sometimes a couple would dance to the tune, or a little toddler would bop up and down whilst holding on to their buggy. So much confidence. They all had confidence, thought Jeanette,

Where had her confidence gone? She was confident when her Fred told her she was a beautiful bride. She was confident in her skills as a mother and at work in the office. She was an excellent office manager. 'The best', they'd said at her retirement party.

All that confidence was gone now, with her children grown, Fred gone and her career over. Part of it was getting older. She knew that a loss of confidence was to be expected, wasn't it? Yet her older sister Lesley wasn't lacking in confidence. She was certainly very confident in her own opinions and quite keen to share them.

"You need to find a new focus, our Jeanette; you're withering away. Fred wouldn't want you to mourn forever. Perhaps there's a new man out there for you."

"No, thank you," I smiled, "I had the best; why on earth would I want to try the rest?"

"Well, a hobby then? You were always good at cakes. What about that? "

"No, thank you. I might have been good at them but didn't enjoy doing them."

Lesley got me thinking, though; I did need a focus. I listened to that piano one day and watched a large gentleman play as his hands danced lightly over the keys. I had wanted to play the piano once. I went for lessons with Mrs Whittam. That was mistake number one; she was a horror, possibly the most critical woman ever to draw breath. I didn't stand a chance. She taught you to play certain pieces but not how to play the piano. I wanted to pick up music and play. I had hoped that would come later. After years of practice, all I got for my trouble was a few lowly piano grades and sore knuckles, where she rapped me with a ruler when I made a mistake. Of course, the more nervous I became, the more mistakes I made.

It all came to a head one day when I was sixteen, it was the summer holidays and I had practised so hard to master this particular piece. Much to my frustration, I made a few mistakes. I saw her reaching for the ruler. I snatched it from her hands and snapped it in two, slamming the lid down on her precious baby grand. I swept out of the room, snatching up her fee as I did so. Thinking about it, it was possibly the only time I ever showed any confidence at all in her music room.

Over fifty years later, I was on the computer when an advert appeared. This new simple way to learn to play the piano. Some sort of App. You learnt the same piece simply at first, then layering it with more difficulty till you got it right. You were working at your own pace. I decided then and there, that would be my focus. I would play the piano again, and this time no rapped knuckles.

I ordered myself an electronic keyboard. I made sure to find one with correctly weighted keys so it felt like a real piano. I spent hours on it with my headphones so the neighbours wouldn't hear. It was my secret. I popped the keyboard in the hall closet whenever the children, grandchildren or my sister came. No one knew.

When I was a girl and played in front of people, my hands shook over the keys. My hands went clammy too. I blamed Mrs Whittam for that, as I always expected painful knuckles to follow any performance. In my little flat on my own with no one to hear, I felt my confidence soar. It wasn't about anyone else. I was doing it for me; when was the last time I did anything just for me? It felt good.

I spent a lot of time in my own little world, playing away. In my younger days, I'd look at the clock, willing for practice time to be over. Now though, the time flew by. I won't lie; it was tricky at first. It was a challenge, but as time passed and with no pressure from anyone, I became proficient. I knew my little repertoire of tunes so well that I could even play them with my eyes closed. I favoured old standards and show tunes, not the classical pieces Mrs Whittam had insisted on.

My favourite was 'On the Sunny Side of the Street'. My Fred used to sing that on the way back from the pub when he'd had a few. It had always made me smile, even if the neighbours weren't quite as appreciative.

I was shopping with Lesley for her latest cruise, somewhere Eastern. I don't know why she bothered, really, because she rarely left the ship. She had to go in 'just one last shop'. I'd waited outside for her when I spied the piano. It was a Monday afternoon and relatively quiet in the precinct. Before I realised what I was doing, I sat at the piano, lifted the lid and started playing. I closed my eyes and played On the Sunny Side of the Street.

I was lost in my own world as if I was still in my little flat. The music lifted my spirits just like it always did. As I played the final notes, I opened my eyes and realised that a small crowd had gathered. At the front of the group was our Lesley, who was proudly telling everyone

"That's my sister."

Suddenly embarrassed, I got up to leave.

"No, you don't, Jeanette. We need to hear another; I need to film it on my phone for the family. They can't miss this. Our Jeanette, the performer, I had no idea."

So, I finished by playing my favourite song from the Sound of Music. No, it wasn't 'Edelweiss' or 'Do-Re-Me'.

I finished by playing 'I Have Confidence' because finally, I really did.

Seaside memories

Back in the day, I hate that term,

We laughed as we walked on the shore.

Lights shone brighter; I can confirm.

Is it wrong to wish for before?

A first date, first love and first kiss

As we cuddled under the pier.

So naive in our youthful bliss,

To know such moments disappear.

I remember this so clearly,

Yet taking my pills slips my mind,

They signal that life is dreary

Years passing can be so unkind.

Lost in time as your hand holds mine

Love and memories intertwine.

Lipstick, Powder and Paint.

I'm on my way. I've made up my mind. I'm breaking up with the woman I love. I know that I will never love anyone as much as I love her. It is simply not possible. What can I tell you about Kari? She's lovely in every way, kind, funny, sensitive, and intelligent. She's faithful too. I haven't come home early to find her in bed with my best mate. We've not had the talk about when she wants to open up the relationship. No, nothing like that. She's not like that.

She's beautiful inside and out, stunning, in fact. Beauty is not normally a drawback in a life partner. In this instance, it is - because I'm not beautiful, not attractive. To be frank, I'm ugly. Even my best friends always called me Shrek or the Beast. She deserves so much better than me; she just hasn't realised it yet. Everyone else has. I see how people look at us when we are out. The incredulity on their faces. Why would she be with him? They cannot get their heads around it.

Only one person thinks we make the perfect couple, and that's my Mum. She doesn't see me as ugly, of course. You've heard the term a face only a mother could love; I'm the proof. She thinks I'm her gorgeous boy. Never has a woman been more biased.

No, one day, Kari will realise that she deserves better; everyone says she will. Every day I love her more; every day it will be harder to let her go and every day will only make it hurt more. I'm not a masochist; this will hurt me like nothing before. It is also an act of my love for her with a huge dollop of self-preservation. So, I've decided to take my broken heart now, please.

Kari and I met at work. It is only a small office; it is only a tiny cosmetics firm, LPP International. The international makes me laugh, as it most certainly isn't. It looks good on the packaging, though. When Kari first started, she just brightened the whole place up. She certainly brightened my days. Not everyone gets my sense of humour, but she did. The days suddenly passed so quickly, with us joking along. The boss was pleased, too, as we seemed to get more done than before. A happy workforce is a productive one.

Don't get me wrong; I found her instantly attractive; who wouldn't? It is not just her looks but her personality and how she interacts with people. I knew that she could never be more than my friend. I had no illusions about that. I was used to being the ugly friend and realised she would never see me that way. We could be pals, though, good pals. I could appreciate her kindness and just being around her. She didn't seem to find my bulk off-putting. People often did, but she didn't.

Strangely children didn't find me off-putting either. They seemed to know that they were safe with me. My Mum calls me the Pied Piper. At family parties, the children would soon be climbing all over me like I was some bouncy castle. If a child gets lost in the supermarket, it will be me that they come to for help. They must sense that I'm just a big softie.

Kari was like that. She had that trust. She remembered everything about me, too. We had a little buffet in the office at Christmastime; she brought everything I liked. She told Mrs Whittam that I couldn't eat her mixed pepper quiche as peppers gave me heartburn. A stupid thing, but she remembered. She cared. She knew me.

It was my birthday that caused the trouble. She bought me a little cake for the office with a candle and everything. A hilarious card and a vintage t-shirt from one of my favourite bands. She got the size right too, which is not easy because I'm big. I was so grateful that I hugged her to say thanks. I expected a quick hug, but she lingered and nestled in my arms. It felt so good, hell, it felt great, but I didn't expect her to sigh. A contented sigh, like she was happy to be there. I suppose it was a safety thing. I'm big, and I make her feel safe. Nothing more. I get it. I think.

Later that afternoon, I mentioned that I was going out with my friends and a couple of their wives and girlfriends.

"You'll be there on your own?"

"Well, I'll be there with them, my pals."

"But they're in couples."

"Well, apart from Rob, He's single too, at the moment, but I'm always on my own, Kari; I'm used to it. I never have a plus one for obvious reasons."

"Obvious reasons?" she queried.

"Have you looked at me?" I laughed, but she didn't. She was remarkably quiet for the rest of the afternoon.

"Enjoy your night," she said in a clipped voice as she reached for her coat.

"Kari, what's wrong? Have I upset you? I am very grateful for everything you've done for my birthday."

"I know you are; it's not that; it's just that I thought we were friends."

"We are. We're more than just colleagues, and I love working with you. You make me laugh like no one else does."

"Well, why are you celebrating your birthday with your other friends but not me?"

"I don't know, I never thought. I didn't think you'd want to. My mates can be pretty full-on, you know? I was trying to protect you and...."

"And?"

"I didn't want to share you."

She smiled at this.

"Well, you don't have to protect me and you won't have to share me either. I'm your friend, but I want to meet your other friends too."

"Will you come then?"

She nodded and I quickly told her where and when. I rang the restaurant to add one more to the reservation."

We were all there on time for once, apart from Kari. I was just about to explain to the group about her when she arrived. She always looked great, of course, but tonight she was breath-taking. Her pale blonde hair was half up and half down. It was in curls; I don't know how she had the time. Her make-up was perfect and the dress seemed to mould to her tiny, perfect figure.

"Wow," said Rob. "It looks like a tiny piece of heaven has just arrived. Yum."

I was just about to tell Rob not to talk about Kari like that. To treat her with the same respect that he treated the other wives and girlfriends, but then I realised I couldn't. She wasn't a wife or girlfriend, but she was my friend and I really didn't like it.

As I processed these thoughts, she came over, put her arm around my waist, and reached up and kissed me on the cheek. She turned and smiled at the shock on my friends' faces.

"Bloody hell," said Rob, "Shrek's pulled."

Everyone laughed, but Kari didn't. Her eyes blazed. I knew that look. It was the same look she had when Barry from accounts accused her of making an error. It turned out that it was Barry's error. It looks like Rob had just made a major error too.

"Yes, Daniel has pulled, as you so inelegantly put it. I prefer to say that I've fallen for him. Don't you ever call him Shrek again in my presence? It's Daniel, Dan or Danny. Now get me a glass of prosecco and we will say no more about it."

Rob looked stunned.

"What about Beast? Can we call him Beast? We've always called him Beast."

"You seem to have a little difficulty understanding me; I'll make it simple. No – you – may – not. Now make that glass of prosecco a bottle. I'll share it with my new friends."

It is a real pity that Rob doesn't move as fast on the five-a-side pitch as he did on his way to the bar. The other three ladies made space in the booth for her.

"We like you already," said one of the girls. I was so stunned that I couldn't tell you who said it.

Apart from Rob looking a bit churlish, we had a great night. I wasn't sure what Kari thought she was doing, but whatever it was, I liked it. I liked it when she defended me. I liked it when she held my hand under the table. I liked it when she climbed on my knee at the end of the night and whispered in my ear,

"Thank you for letting me come. I don't want this to stop."

Seeing us cuddled together was obviously too much for Rob and he turned to the rest of the table.

"This is ridiculous. What on earth could someone like her, see in Shrek..., I mean Danny. She's gorgeous, a bit of a grumpy cow, but gorgeous. What would she see in him? Is she doing it for a bet?"

The rest of my friends looked shocked. I don't think he expected Kari to hear, but she did.

"That's why you are going home on your own, Rob. For a bet? Don't judge others by your low standards. You really don't get it at all, do you?

Well, I can promise you that Daniel here is most definitely going to get it tonight."

With that, she jumped off my knee and led me to the waiting taxi, to the cheers of the rest of the table.

I sat stunned in the cab.

"You almost had me believing all that back there. I wish...."

"You wish what?"

It must have been the drink that made me say it before I could stop myself.

"That it was true. That you were coming back to mine."

"I am, but I can't stay all night. Long enough to give you your real birthday present anyway."

That's what she did too. She came home with me. She took me by the hand and asked where the bathroom was. I waited on the bed in my t-shirt and boxers. When she appeared in the doorway, she found the room in darkness. She looked for the switch.

"No, I said. I don't want you to see me. I'm big and podgy and lumpy."

She found the light and flicked it on.

"Well, I want to see all of you. Maybe I like podgy and lumpy. Now, what was this big stuff you were talking about?"

I couldn't answer as I couldn't speak. I was struck dumb by the perfection I was looking at. She was pale, and her skin seemed to glow in the light. She was so beautiful that I felt guilty about touching her with my big, ugly hands. Not too guilty that I didn't, however. I might be big and ugly, but I am not stupid.

I was surprised when Kari whispered that I was her first. I had been with a few different women who weren't that discerning. I'd had sex, but I had never made love, until now.

"I saved myself for someone special. I am so glad it is you."

Afterwards, we cuddled and she rested her hand on my chest.

"Is it always that good?" she sighed.

"If you are with the right person, it must be, because I have never experienced anything as good," I replied, smiling.

We dozed and then she got up to leave.

"Stay. Please. Don't go." I said, reaching for her. I saw her hesitate for a second.

"No, I've got to go; I said I would."

"So, my birthday is well and truly over then. That's it?" I said petulantly.

"You are a stupid man at times, Daniel Hamelin. I've waited months for you to ask me out. I've dreamed about it. Now, it's happened after I made it happen. Don't think for a second that I'm letting you go because I'm not. I'll be back in the morning. I'm bringing breakfast; now sleep."

With that, she kissed me on the forehead and was gone. Don't tell anyone, but I slept on her pillow. It smelt of her perfume. Big soft devil, I am. As I drifted off to sleep, I was already thinking about how much this would hurt when she came to her senses.

She was back at 9.00 am, with breakfast from my favourite coffee shop.

"I thought I'd let you sleep in. I thought that you might need the rest after last night."

My dream girl was here looking all perky and gorgeous and she had brought coffee and muffins from my favourite coffee shop. I just smiled at her. How did my life get so good? This morning her hair was in this headband thing and she was wearing purple. Purple may be my new favourite colour.

"So, Daniel, how are you feeling?"

"Happy, scared, shocked, but mostly happy."

"Why shocked? You must have known that I liked you. We get on brilliantly."

"We do; you're wonderful. I love being with you, but I never thought you would like me as anything other than mates."

"I don't understand why? You must have had some inkling that I was interested in you."

With that, I gently stood her in front of the mirror. She seemed so delicate, standing in front of me, talk about beauty and the beast. Rob was right.

"Look at me, then look at you. We don't look right together. Why would someone as gorgeous as you want to go out with me?"

She looked sad as she looked into my eyes.

"Do you want to know what I see? I see the kindest, funniest, gentlest man I've ever known. I see a man I saved myself for. I also see his lovely smile and his gorgeous eyes that look like chocolate buttons. Turn around."

We swapped places in the mirror so that I was standing in front of her.

"I also see the cutest, roundest, sexiest bottom I've ever seen. When you walked to the bathroom in the night, I was quite mesmerised."

With that, she slapped my buttocks rather hard. I quite liked it.

"No more talk of you not being good enough. I find it very annoying when people insult my man. That includes when he does it to himself."

"Is that what I am then, your man?" I laughed, still in shock.

"Yes, and don't you forget it." She said as she came in for another one of those amazing hugs.

Things just went from strength to strength. We spent so much time together. My Mum loved her and as it was nearly Christmas when our relationship changed, she was soon included in family parties. My best mate Callum and his wife Michelle loved her too. They were happy to see me so content. I was, but I still had so many doubts. When I was with Kari, everything was wonderful. I never doubted her feelings for me. When we were apart, the doubts came. They came in hard and tackled any rational thought. You know that feeling when you wake up at 3.00 am and your worries seem to magnify and multiply? It was like that. It was like that whenever we were apart.

There were so many unanswered questions. She'd never stay the night at my place. She always left me sleeping. I had never met any of her friends or family. Was she that ashamed of me? I'd never even been allowed to visit her flat. She lived with her friend Coral who let Kari live there practically rent-free. They shared one bedroom and Kari said it wasn't fair to Coral to invade her limited space. She didn't want to rock the boat.

There were so many red flags and they bothered me so much. She wouldn't go away with me; I wanted us to have a weekend somewhere. I wanted to wake up with her. Yes, I'm a big softie, but I think that you have probably already worked that out. Going away was a no-go. Why did she not want to be seen with me at a hotel? She seemed to have no problem with being seen anywhere else with me. It was me that had the problem with that sometimes. I saw people's surprised looks and their sniggers. We were at a lovely restaurant when I almost hit some bloke after I saw him silently mouth the word "Escort" to his companion. You see, that was what strangers thought, that someone as lovely as Kari would only be with me if I were paying for her company. I never told Kari that one; there was no use in both of us being upset. I did tell her that we got some odd looks, but she just laughed it off. She genuinely didn't see the problem, but I did. She did everything she could to make me feel loved that I forgot everything else when we were together.

The niggles wouldn't go away, however. There was always someone like Rob, keen to have a bit of banter and feed my insecurities. Insecurities that hadn't mattered until I fell in love, I tried to distance myself from Rob and some of my other more vocal mates, but they got into my head.

I think the final straw was when Callum, who I trusted so much, said,

"I think she is a lovely girl, mate and you're obviously smitten, but where is this relationship going? She won't stay over or go away with you? I think you're right; there are a lot of red flags and as lovely as she is, she's definitely hiding something.

You've not even been to her flat or met this, Coral. For all you know, she could be shacked up with a bloke."

He must have seen my face,

"I hope she isn't, mate, but it is all a bit odd. I'd love to tell you that you were being paranoid, but I don't think you are."

I knew that Callum, unlike some of my mates, only had my best interests at heart. No, this won't do; I'm going round to her flat, which I've never been allowed to visit and stop this once and for all. I'll take my heartbreak now, please. If this Coral exists, she will be there to support her after I've gone.

I soon found the right door. I rang the bell and this guy answered; this very handsome guy stripped to the waist. He had a wonderful physique. He was everything that I wasn't. He was everything she deserved. I looked at him and said,

"I'm sorry, I think I've got the wrong door. I was looking for Kari. Sorry for disturbing you."

I turned to go and Mr Handsome said,

"No, wait. She's here Daniel. I'll get her for you. She's just in the bedroom."

I carried on walking. Well, it was more of a jog, to be fair. I needed to get away. Well, I said I wanted my heartbreak now and I got my wish. I just didn't think that it would hurt this much. Why let me fall in love with her when all the time she had this hunk?

I managed to get to a park and sank down onto a bench. A few minutes later, I was joined by Mr Handsome.

"Bloody hell Daniel, for a big lad, you can certainly pick up some speed. I barely had a chance to catch up with you."

I didn't even look at him, stared straight ahead and spoke,

"Look, I don't even know who you are, but I really don't feel like talking at the moment. Just leave me alone to let my heart break in peace."

"Oh love, and they say I'm a Drama Queen. Stop adding up 2 and 2 and making 27. I suggest you listen to what I have to say. I'm Coral, original name Carl. Don't ever use that, please. I'm Kari's best friend in the whole world, apart from you. I'm also her family and most importantly, her fairy Godfather. I granted all her wishes and I'm about to grant some of yours too."

I just stared at him as he carried on,

"Well, I'm obviously no threat to your relationship, am I? I'm on your side, promise."

"Why keep you a secret then? "I blurted out, "Why lie?"

"It wasn't me that she was keeping a secret, silly boy. She does have secrets, but she hasn't told you any lies, really. I told her to be honest with you, or she'd end up hurting you both. I'd just about convinced her, too, then you turned up looking all wounded. Come on back with me and sort all this out once and for all."

Walking back in silence together, I realised that Coral had dropped behind slightly. I stopped and turned.

"She's right; you have got a lovely bum," he laughed.

I didn't know quite how to react to that.

When we got back to the flat, Kari was in the lounge. It was a lovely flat, all creams with flecks of gold here and there. Above the fireplace was a large portrait of a glamorous lady who bore more than a passing resemblance to Coral. I could barely look at Kari and she just hung her head.

"Come on Kari," said Coral, "tell your man your secrets. You've been very silly. I told you that he loves you. The poor lad was breaking his heart when he saw me. I don't mind being a heartbreaker normally, but we can't break his Kari. He's too special. Now, you two, I'll be in the kitchen making us brunch. I'll have the radio on and I'll be rattling pans, so I won't be able to hear anything. I do expect to hear all later, though."

With that, he was gone. He was a force of nature. I couldn't help but like him. I'd love to introduce him to Rob and see them interact.

Kari looked at me. Her eyes were brimming with tears. I couldn't bear it. I held her gently.

"Daniel, I'm going to tell you everything, but I need you to promise not to interrupt. Can you do that?

I nodded and so, slowly, she told me her story.

"I've always been slight. I was also very plain—baby fine, pale blonde hair. I could never grow it to any length. It frustrated my Mum. She wanted a pretty daughter to dress up, with plaits. She could dress me up, but I never looked right. Pale hair, pale skin. Eyebrows and eyelashes were so light they looked non-existent. They called me the mouse. I was so quiet and shy, even with the closest family. They didn't want me. I was a burden. I got in the way of their social life. My mum and stepfather didn't have much money, but they liked to socialise. They liked a drink. Eventually, their love of booze became all-consuming.

Being a teenager living with two alcoholics was not fun. There was no escape at school, either. I was bullied there too. I was such an easy target. I was so plain that I provided ammunition for their cruel words. I was the mouse to them, too. They told me that no one would ever love me or find me attractive. Why would they?

When I was 17, I started working with Coral in a fancy dress shop. It really appealed to me, dressing up, becoming someone else. Someone other than me. Someone who wasn't the mouse. Coral and I hit it off. I finally felt that I had someone in my life who cared about me. He told me that he did drag as Madame Coral at weekends. He was only just starting out then. I desperately wanted to see him perform, but I was 17 and looked 13. No one was going to let me go in a club. So that was when he worked his magic on me. Full make-over or glow up as he called it. The aim was to make me look older; what I didn't expect was to look pretty. Apart from my hair, which still looked rubbish, I looked good for the first time ever.

He is a master with makeup. He gave the little mouse features, eyelashes, eyebrows, lips and cheekbones. Just enough to make it look almost natural. He even sorted out my hair too. He put on this hairpiece, a ¾ wig. The hairline was my own hair but the rest was not. I looked and felt amazing. This new person that I never imagined I could be. People treated me differently, too. They were so kind to me when I looked good. It felt amazing.

I loved watching Coral perform and I felt happy. I felt like me, the me I should have been. A few weeks later, as my confidence grew, there was a particularly nasty argument with my mum. She didn't like the little mouse changing. I think in her drink-addled brain; she was jealous. She hit me hard. She broke a cheekbone. I ran to the only friend that I had in the world. Coral. I never went back. I've been here ever since, being loved and looked after by him. He's my big brother, mother and father all rolled into one."

She paused to gather her thoughts,

"Why have I never met him then if he's your family? Was I not important enough to you?"

"Of course, you were. I was building up to it, but I knew I couldn't keep my secret once you met him. You would have to meet the little mouse."

"I don't understand."

"Daniel, I fell in love with you, but you fell in love with Kari. The pretty girl. I knew you weren't shallow, but I was. I still had enough insecurity to be scared that you wouldn't love the real me. I still am."

I just looked at her; I was amazed at what she had told me. I was also so annoyed that she hadn't trusted me. That she hadn't understood how much I loved her, not how she looked.

"Kari, I don't love you because of how you look. I love you because you're kind and funny and make me laugh like no one else. I love you because you are clever and smart and you are always on my side. Of course, I think you are beautiful, but that's just incidental to me. If anything, that's your only fault in my eyes. It scares me that you're so beautiful and I'm not. I love you and if anything, I think I love you even more now that I know what you have been through. You've got to trust me."

"Why – you didn't trust me. You didn't trust that I loved you. You couldn't believe me because if how you look."

"You're right; my insecurities nearly ruined the best thing that ever happened to me. Your insecurities nearly did too. Do you know how much it hurts me when you won't stay overnight? How much it hurts me when you leave?"

"I wanted to stay. I always want to stay with you, but if I'd stayed, you would have to have seen me when I look like the little mouse. I couldn't risk losing you."

"Well, I want to see the little mouse now. I think I may like her."

She looked uncertain but knew that it was no longer an option. She got up and went to the bedroom. Coral appeared and put a coffee next to me.

"I've done you a coffee like I like my men – hot, black and strong."

With that he disappeared again and went back to rattling his pans.

After what seemed like hours, but was probably just minutes, I heard a slight cough behind me and there was Kari. She had no makeup on at all, her long hair had gone and her own hair was in a tiny knot at the back of her head.

She was still the most beautiful thing I had ever seen. I held out my arms and told her just that. I held her all the time, telling her that I loved her and thought she was just as lovely as I ever had.

It seemed that I was the Pied Piper after all, only this time, there were no rats involved; I'd just captured the heart of a little mouse.

With that, the door to the kitchen was flung open and Coral appeared with Eggs Benedict for brunch.

"Finally," he said, "I thought I would have to bang your heads together. I was thinking in the kitchen what a fabulous Uncle I will be when you two have babies. How many would you like? I'd like three."

He wasn't disappointed; we did go on to have three children together. Coral loves to tell people that was so we could have one each. He was right; he was the best uncle and friend to Kari and me. Our three children adored him. I know what you are thinking: what did the children look like? Well, they got Karis's delicate features and my dark colouring; they are gorgeous, but I might be biased.

As for Kari, she continues to be as lovely as ever. I love the idea that only I get the privilege of seeing the real her, and waking up with her every morning is always a treat. Though most mornings these days, we also get to wake up with at least one child and a dog too.

You know I don't care what anyone thinks of how I look now because she picked me and that is all that matters. I did hear someone ask Kari recently why someone that looked like her was with me. After singing my praises as a father, husband and lover, she said;

"Besides, you should see me without makeup. It's quite frightening. Trust me; it's just lipstick powder and paint."

Julie

I'm sat on a dog's ball, balanced on a vase. The ball is clean; it's not covered in dog slobber. If I'm any judge, she's washed it in fairy liquid. The dog won't want it back. He's dead. He was called Perry after

Perry Como. She listens to his songs all the time. I heard her tell her mate, Mrs Atkinson from next door, that she's had six dogs called Perry all in all. Four corgis and two Jack Russells. All with the same name. Fancy. Apparently, it was a lot easier to remember and until they moved, they could re-use the dog tag.

Names are funny things, aren't they? I'm a Julie Petite. There's a lot of us about—all different colours, from black to white and every shade in between. There are even different constructions. There's the basic cap at the cheaper end of the market and then there's me, the Julie petite hand-tied monofilament. I wouldn't say I like to brag, but I am top-end. There are not many like me living in a one-bed warden-controlled council flat. No, my sisters are holidaying in the Algarve, possibly well-secured on a yacht. At night they are laid to rest on a proper stand, maybe with a silk scarf draped over them to protect their delicate fibres. No, there's only one like me, stuck in a flat with a blind OAP, sitting on a dead dog's ball.

I didn't mention that she was blind, did I? Of course, I have every sympathy, but it is a fate worse than death for a top-quality hairpiece to be owned by a blind person. She'll never get my fringe right, will she? Never position my delicate lace front with care. She just plonks me on like I'm some bobble hat. She tries her best, I suppose, but it's just guesswork, really.

Her son bought me. He's got money. They scrimped and saved to get him to university and off he went, never to return. He married a model. Well, he tells everyone he married a model. She sat on an Austin Allegro in a bikini for a week at the motor show in 1973, so I suppose that counts. Of course, she's knocking on a bit now. She's had her face lifted. I heard the blind one telling Mrs Atkinson. Of course, she couldn't see it, but she felt the scars behind her ears.

It was the son who insisted that she had me. He only comes down a couple of times a year. He couldn't take her out with a few tufts on top of her head, could he? You can't keep a nylon headscarf on at a nice steakhouse, can you? Wear me and I'll take you anywhere. You can part me wherever you want.

My colour is shaded pearl. It's quite a sophisticated hue. I'm often admired – especially when her nephew or his wife calls. They look after me. Give me a wash and a condition. I always look fabulous if they're here to put me on her. Better than the picture in the catalogue. They're both theatricals; he's got a degree in it. He used to brush out the wigs in his university productions. I like that boy. A little shake and fluff from him and I'm looking my best and then, of course, so is she.

I shouldn't be hard on her. She's a lovely woman and I'd certainly rather be on her head than this ball, believe you me. I'll be stuck on here for days now. She's not going out till next Tuesday, a doctor's appointment. Mrs Atkinson goes with her. Her hair is all her own. It's the exact same shade as a brillo pad. I think she's jealous of me. I can see it in her eyes.

The priest comes to visit sometimes. She pops me on for him. He's a lovely young man. He'd be shocked to hear the language she uses when she's watching the horse racing. I can't imagine where she learnt words like that – she used to work in a sweet shop. She tried to carry on as her sight was fading, but she kept giving pear drops to people who'd asked for Everton mints, so she had to go.

Oh, there's the bell. It's that lovely nephew. He's got her a present. Hang on. He hasn't got her a present; he's got me one. He's lifting me up. He's got lovely soft hands. What's he putting me on? It's a head, a lovely cool polystyrene head. It's remarkably comfortable. I've got a face, a pretty, delicate, perfect little face.

I knew I liked that boy.

Gran's Seaside Shenanigans

Gran lost her teeth on the Ferris Wheel,

Out they flew, everyone heard the squeal.

Kiddies paddling in the pool just ran,

The Fair boss gave Gran a lifetime ban.

A dental adventure's not ideal,

We must find them; let's launch an appeal.

To search everywhere, that was the plan,

Under the pier and the ice cream van.

How poor Gran wished her teeth were still real,

With only gums, you can't be genteel.

"A seagull swooped with a huge wing span

And took Gran's teeth," said the deckchair man.

Without her teeth, Gran lost all her zeal,

Soup has become her favourite meal.

Just Like Old Times

Joanne is 56; she is dressed to impress. She is holding a large glass of wine as she talks.

I didn't want to come to this school reunion. It's been a long time—forty years since we left. A school reunion, it's very American, isn't it? Like Halloween, in my day, it was a hollowed-out turnip. Now it's wall-to-wall pumpkins.

I sound like such an old woman, don't I? I'm not. I'm 56. Mind you, that was old when I was young. Then 56-year-old women had curly grey perms like the queen, thick glasses and a pleated skirt. Now they have long hair, contact lenses and a mini dress.

I have made a big effort for tonight; hair curled with a few lash extensions. This dress is very flattering. Thankfully no one can see the foundation garment I'm wearing to hold it all in. Trust me; it doesn't flatter on its own.

I know I'm vain, but I was nervous about tonight. I needed to give myself an extra bit of confidence. Seeing the change in people is lovely, but I didn't want to have changed that much. I wanted to be recognisable.

I know I should count my blessings. I've got a wonderful loving husband and family. My career in journalism might have been small, but I've helped people and had a sense of achievement.

At least I've not been in prison like Jane Smart. She isn't here tonight. She doesn't get out for another three years.

The reunion is in a hotel because they knocked our school down in 1994 to build a housing estate.

My friend Melanie lives there. She's never forgiven me for telling her that her conservatory was built on the site of the boy's urinals. Well, it was.

You know, I don't know why I worried. I'm having a great time. Everyone says I haven't changed a bit. It's almost like old times.

Compound Fractures

Don't just be a pot

You have the power

To be a flower.

Don't just be cold stone

It's time to show them

You are a true gem

Don't just be mere crumbs

You must strive ahead

Aim to be the bread

Don't just be on time

Avoiding any strife

Be early in life.

Don't just be the beat

Listen to me, chum

You can be the drum

Don't just be a shell

You're anything but

Be the coconut

Don't just be the storm

You will not blunder

Show them your thunder.

Don't just be a flash

Briefly shining bright

Beam a constant light.

Don't just be the lace

Show what you can do

Be a sturdy shoe.

Don't just be un wise

Following the flock

Make time off the clock.

Custard

Nick is 52. He is sitting at a table in an Italian restaurant. He's wearing a polo-neck jumper.

Well, it's all been a bit of a rush, truth be told. I hate rushing. I'm never late, always on time, but I pace myself. The trick is to give yourself enough time and it's always worked for me until now. Now time is definitely the issue. Not enough time.

To look at me, you wouldn't know. I look the best I've looked for years. The irony! I've just lost 50 pounds in the last six months at my slimming club. I'm their Mr Smooth this year. I had to pose for photos in my new slimline suit, wearing a sash, like some sort of beauty queen. Thankfully, there wasn't a swimwear section. I don't know who was more relieved about that, me or the girls in the club. I'm only Mr Smooth for my branch, of course. I don't tend to mention that I'm the only man that goes to my branch, either. Even so, it's an achievement. My Natalie is very proud of me, but I do wish that she wouldn't tell everyone that her husband is "male member of the year". She's that innocent. She never gets why they smirk.

Bless her; how a mother of two strapping teenage boys can be so innocent beats me. I listen to the kids, explaining things to her. It is hilarious sometimes. She'll be the star of a Tik Tok before long, no doubt.

I just hope that I'm here to see it.

She's trying to be brave. Stoic, I think, is the word they use. She's smiling and laughing, but I can tell she's worried.

I didn't really react when I got the news. I need this operation tomorrow urgently. I've got the top consultant; they call her the Queen of Surgery, the consultant's consultant. I'm very lucky, in a way. I've got the best. Turns out I need the best. It is going to be a very tricky and long operation. They warned me I might not survive it. I suppose they say that to everyone, don't they? Covering themselves, I suppose. Worst case scenario and all that. Anyway, it's not like I have much choice, is it? Two months to live without the operation, they reckon. Now, that was a shock.

It's only my thyroid, my perfectly functioning, if not attractive, thyroid. The problem is, is that it's big, it's grown like a triffid and it's crushing my windpipe. Crushed to a pinprick in places. They were amazed I'd not collapsed. I think it's because I've not been doing so much since my breathing got worse.

Anyway, I'm here with the family at the Italian restaurant, our Jacob's joked,

"It's the condemned man's last supper."

We all laughed. We love a bit of gallows humour. Not our Liam, though; he's taking it hard. He's gone in on himself, I can tell.

I tried to cheer everyone up. It is what it is. We haven't any choice. We have to trust that all will be well. We do have a choice to have a good time tonight, though, and that's what I'm going to do.

I've missed pasta and creamy sauces. I've missed bread and cheese and custard. I love custard so much. Oh, I've missed custard. I've missed wine too, but of course, I can't have that tonight, the night before the op. Custard. Now that I can have.

I've been so good with my diet. I'm going to have whatever I want tonight. Forget the calories.

Jake is trying to get Liam to smile. He's not succeeding.

Natalie takes my hand as I finish my second dessert. She looks at me and doesn't say a word. That look tells me all I need to know. She's telling me that she sees through my bravado. She knows I'm scared. She's telling me that she needs me to be OK.

I smile back and simply say,

"I love you more than custard."

I'm a little teacup.

Ooh, you've got cold hands.

It was warm in the cupboard. I like it in the dark; it's peaceful.

Be gentle, don't bang me on the worktop.

What are you filling me with today? I like hot chocolate myself.

Don't even think of black coffee, it leaves a dirty ring.

I like that raspberry fruit tea, too, it's refreshing.

Oh, it's normal tea. Here comes the hot stuff.

I don't like the tea bag. She's a bitch.

She likes to take over. Her flavour seeps into my earthenware.

That's it, squeeze the old bag, throw her in the bin.

Cool me down with some cold milk. Full fat?

I would have thought that skimmed milk would be wise.

Oh well, no one listens to me. Sugar too? You are cheeky.

Where are we going to? In the conservatory? Ooh, that's posh.

Sip me slowly. Enjoy. Oh, you're done. That's quick.

Clean me by hand; you've got time. I want that lovely bubbly bath.

No, not the machine. It's noisy and the plates are so dirty and common.

I'm just glad that they've got their own cupboard.

As for the cutlery. I'm glad they go in a drawer.

Oh well, it's jacuzzi time.

Battle Lines Drawn

Always one to avoid a fight,
Now in a battle with my plight.

It took time for anger to grow
I fought against an unknown foe.

Without warning, a new disease
Took my health, brought me to my knees.

The medics had no magic wand.
Blind to why it didn't respond.

All they'd learnt, all they thought they knew.
Now just clueless, like me or you.

Others tried hard to sympathise
When they saw the pain in our eyes.

How can you explain the fatigue?
Tiredness that is a whole new league.

Exertion makes you lose your breath,
Gasping for air, scares you to death.

Pain will set every joint aflame.
Your life will never be the same.

Career has gone and no return.
Long empty days are my concern.

The fever left a damaged brain.
Sent my intellect down the drain.

Words float away when I'm speaking.
From here, memories are leaking.

Life is small, no independence.
Depression is in ascendance.

You cannot walk or dance or run,
Is it easy to buy a gun?

No, you must fight to save what's left.
Now's not the time to feel bereft.

It's vital to guard your castle,
Though the fight will be a hassle.

Another sunset, almost here,
Try to face the night without fear.

Time to sleep; your bed is calling.
Sleep well; your eyelids are falling.

The portcullis is coming down,
Hide all your pain, don't show your frown.

With each new dawn, you may conquer
Life is too precious to squander.

Grandma's Button Tin

My Gran never had much, but she used to say that she was the wealthiest woman she knew. She had her memories and she had lots of love.

"Not everyone can say that my sweetheart," she used to say.

She certainly had a lot of love from me, her only grandson. I loved spending time with her in her little flat more than anything else. She'd tell me stories, the people she'd met, all the things she'd seen. She had never been to another country. She didn't even visit London until she was almost 70. Even though she wasn't well travelled, her stories were so vivid; it felt like I was there. There at that first dance with my grandad in the 1930s. I could hear the music playing. I could hear the chairs scraping across the floor as they got up to dance. I was there. It was like that with all her stories.

She used to get out the big photo album if she needed a prompt. Of course, that illustrated the stories differently. It gave all those long-departed friends and relatives faces in my head as she told their tales. The best story prompt, though, was her button tin. Outside, the tin was worn and brown, with only the faded image of what had once been. Inside, the lid was still shiny and bright, showing a bluebird flying across the orange unscratched paint. Bluebird Toffee Luxury Assortment, it stated proudly. This didn't detract from the real treasure - the buttons shining within - buttons of all colours, textures and sizes.

I spent hours with those buttons, counting and sorting them into different classifications. Colour and size, obviously, but then the number of holes.

"All the twos over there, Gran, all the fours there."

As I got older, the classifications became even more complicated. The ordinary everyday buttons: the black and the pearl ones, were good to sort. The shiny metal ones were fun too, but the special ones were my favourite as they prompted the stories.

Whilst I sorted, Gran would tell me the stories of the buttons. The tiny pale blue satin ones that had been on the cuffs of her wedding dress. Her something blue. Her eyes were always misted over when she talked about that. She only had one wedding photo and it had been coloured by hand. She always used to complain that her headpiece wasn't on straight,

"You'd have thought my Mam would have sorted it."

The big fat pink buttons covered in nylon were cut from an old dressing gown. That always prompted the story of how she nearly died from peritonitis and the relief she'd felt that she'd had a decent dressing gown, despite the emergency.

Not all of the buttons were loose in the tin. Wrapped in tissue paper, two little yellow duck-shaped buttons were still attached to the card they came on. They came from a cardigan Gran had knitted for me when I was tiny.

There were the big fat leather-covered buttons. They were from a cardigan that Grandad had worn at home. He was a smart man, my grandad. He would never wear a cardigan outside, always a suit, collar and tie. Although he had died before I was born, I'd seen the photos in the album. Photos of him sitting on the beach in his suit and hat, although he had taken his shoes off to show willing. As I held these buttons, I used to feel closer to him, like I was holding a part of him. Gran used to watch my face as though she was reading my thoughts,

"He would have thought that you were a little smasher, you know. He'd be that proud of you."

I hoped that was true. There were other buttons, too. The biggest one of all was the fur one. It wasn't real fur, of course. It was huge, almost like a side plate. It was from the coat my Gran had worn when Mum and Dad married. It had a wrap-around collar that was fastened with this huge button.

"I looked very smart that day, even if I say so myself." Gran smiled as she stroked the fur backwards and forwards across the button.

The only problem was that sometimes the tin was used for its actual purpose and I sometimes found that a friend or neighbour had plundered it for some buttons for a matinee jacket or something. I always knew when something was missing. I think I sensed it. However, Gran ensured that only the everyday, ordinary buttons were taken. Nothing that was special to her or me.

When I needed a rest from my sorting, I had my favourite of all favourites to play with, the roll of elastic. It had been purchased decades ago for a long-forgotten project. It had been rolled up for so long that you could unwind it and it would roll back into place. It didn't matter how many times you did it. It went back exactly the same. My mum watched me playing with it once and seeing the joy on my face, said,

"Mam, all the toys he's got and I swear he gets more pleasure from that bit of old elastic." She was right; I did.

I lost Gran when I was 22, almost 30 years ago now. I still miss her every day. I suspect I always will. I never realised as a small boy what I was learning from those old buttons and elastic, but most importantly from Gran. The buttons and elastic taught me that value wasn't always measured in how much something cost. That real treasure could be found in the simplest things: a job well done, an early walk on a summer's morning or finishing the last clue in the crossword. Gran taught me to value the people we meet along the way, to collect their stories and to remember and share our own with those who want to listen. Most importantly, she taught me to treasure those we love.

Albert's Eggs

Albert set the table for two. He used the floral placemats that Lillian liked best. The cutlery was the last remaining pieces from their wedding canteen. Still, two place settings left after 63 years of marriage, enough for the two of them. He couldn't make much, but Albert was good with eggs: scrambled, poached, boiled but never fried. What was it that Lillian always said?

"Why make something good for you unhealthy?"

Albert always made breakfast, and Lillian did all the other cooking.

Boiled eggs today. He shuffled from the sink to the hob. He was not as steady on his feet as he used to be. He timed the eggs carefully. Lillian liked hers soft, but not too soft,

"Just the right amount of dippy for me, Albert," she always said.

He put them in the egg cups, the ones they got on holiday. Hers was shaped like an old car with running boards and a starting handle. His was shaped like a donkey, the egg sitting in a basket on its back.

The toast was already buttered and cut into soldiers. He placed them on the table. Then he remembered. Lillian wouldn't be eating her breakfast today. She wouldn't be eating breakfast any day.

Albert was brought up during the war with rationing. He couldn't waste it. He'd just eat both. That's what he did, as a solitary tear dripped into the yolk.

My Postman

My postman's got cataracts.

I don't like to complain.

But it makes things so awkward.

It's becoming a pain.

All the letters and parcels

Disappear down the lane.

Yes, most of them do come back.

Don't lose much in the main.

But, poor old Mrs Richards,

Won't go out in the rain.

"If wet, wait till tomorrow!"

She has made that quite plain.

I can't say that I blame her,

But I'd like to abstain.

"Too busy to do his job,"

Is a constant refrain.

I don't speak to number 12.

Binned, their mail will remain.

I just won't darken their door.

Rage I've had to restrain.

What she said about mother.

Involved using cocaine.

Mum won't even have Lemsip.

My neighbour is insane.

I've stopped bidding on Ebay

It's just not worth the strain.

Of all the missing parcels,

And it's not that I'm vain.

But I don't want my neighbours

Treating me with disdain,

Because I bought bleaching cream

The moustache back again.

I do have some sympathy,

I try to be humane

But he must be efficient.

He can't just have free reign.

So, I'm off to head office.

Who knows there what I'll gain?

I don't want him in trouble.

Maybe he can retrain?

If there's no satisfaction,

I will start a campaign.

Actually, his boss was kind,

Handsome and quite urbane.

He simply agreed with me,

We couldn't entertain

This carrying on longer

Too tricky to sustain.

So, postie is on light duties,

I hope, not too mundane.

It won't be long till his op,

Then back to his domain.

Now we've got a replacement,

My mood is down the drain.

It's the bitch from number 12,

My wrath I won't contain.

Overlooking the Park

The problem with Mandy was that she really didn't listen. She looked like she was listening, but she wasn't. She might pick the things that she thought were important but couldn't be guaranteed to remember them.

She was scatter-brained; it was part of her charm, but it sometimes frustrated me. After 12 years of marriage, I'd learnt to love all her foibles. We had fun together and were best friends. I couldn't have loved her more.

I was good at showing it, too. For a big bluff guy, I tried my best to be romantic, with lots of gifts, flowers and not just on special occasions. She drove the new car and I drove the old banger.

I wasn't bothered about having a flash car, a big house or material things. That was for her because they made her happy. Happy wife, happy life and all that.

I earned good money, but it wasn't the most glamorous job. I worked in the warehouse; I was the distribution manager of a large confectionary business. I had a huge staff but a little windowless office. Due to health and safety rules, I also had to wear boots, a hard hat and a high-vis jacket on the warehouse floor.

Mandy was not impressed with that; she wanted me to wear a suit with a nice office with windows overlooking the park. I'd explained that most of those suits didn't earn as much and were lower down the food chain than me, but she didn't listen.

My work Christmas party was legendary. Our bosses were very generous, a beautiful hotel and everyone from the lowliest worker on the shop floor to the Chairman attended.

Mandy and I and always loved these occasions. She loved the chance to get dressed up and I loved the opportunity to show off my beautiful wife. I also loved to dance with Mandy, to hold her in my arms on the dance floor.

We had a rule, no dancing with anyone else. That's why I was shocked last Christmas to come back from the bar to see Mandy dancing with Jason Kent. Although she had broken our rule, it wouldn't have bothered me too much, but this was a slow dance. I wasn't going to sit there and watch him run his hands over my Mandy. I cut in and said,

"Thank you for looking after my wife whilst I was stuck at the bar, Jason. I'm back now. You can go."

I think something in my tone ensured that Jason didn't argue. Mandy knew I was angry.

"You didn't have to do that; he was only being kind."

"Yes, kind enough to get his hands on my wife. Don't think everyone didn't see where those hands were roaming, either. You broke our rule; you didn't have to do that."

It was very quiet at home for a few days until I calmed down, and things seemed to return to normal.

It was February when Stan, one of the older men in the warehouse, came to see me. I respected him.

"Look, boss, there's no easy way to say this, but your wife is seeing Jason Kent. I've heard some of the lads talking about it. They wanted to sort him out; they are loyal to you. They gave me this."

With that, he passed me his phone. There was a video of Jason and Mandy in her car. Let's just say they had progressed from slow dancing. I thanked Stan for his loyalty and to tell the lads to do what they felt they had to but not to get into trouble on my account.

After Stan left, I requested a full audit of Jason's orders. I am very popular in the accounts department. It didn't take long to find enough discrepancies to have him dismissed.

Mandy seemed pleased when she came home to find me wearing a suit.

"Have you had good news at work? Have they finally promoted you?"

"No, Mandy. I wore the suit to see the solicitor; I'm divorcing you."

"Divorce? Why?"

"If you don't know, perhaps Jason can help you understand?"

"Jason? But I did that for us. For you. I didn't even enjoy it. He said he could get you an office overlooking the park, out of that awful warehouse."

"That awful warehouse paid for all this, Mandy. How was Jason going to help me get a promotion? I'm his boss's boss!"

The problem with Mandy was that she really didn't listen.

A Bloody Battle

It's a bloody battle of will,

No matter how many tears spill,

At times a childish playground fight,

He said, she said, but who is right?

But of course, you don't really care

It's psychological warfare.

Went to the top to fight my case.

But of course, you laughed in my face.

The truth can never be a lie.

You will no longer make me cry.

But of course, you don't really care.

It's psychological warfare.

But if I do not win the fight.

I'll keep trying with all my might.

So, I will kick and scream and shout.

Morally right, there is no doubt.

So continues my silent prayer.

It's psychological warfare.

The Cave

I'm sitting in front of Abanazers's cave. I won't go in; I'm not as easily tricked as Aladdin. I couldn't if I wanted to as it is just a piece of scenery. The grey stones of the cave were painted long ago. Other pieces of scenery are piled up behind it on the left side of the stage. I can see a glimpse of Rene's café from 'Allo 'Allo!, the hatch from Dinner Ladies and the stained glass window from the Vicar of Dibley. Above me in the dusty gloom are wires and ropes and strings. I don't know what they do; it's all a bit technical for me.

I can see a spinning wheel; is it from Sleeping Beauty? No, I look again; it's the wheel from a ship; it is surprising how many pantomimes involve a sea journey in the second act. Well, they do have those tropical costumes to get their money's worth from. In front of me, I see my costumes. They are hanging on some abandoned upended rostra. Shirts, ties, but most excitingly, a white sailor costume with Velcro fastenings to facilitate a quick change.

There's a door currently blocked by staging in front. It has an accessible peephole to spy on the audience; I hide unseen as they enter. I hear their chatter. They are smiling, that's good. Smiling is only one step away from laughing. Please let them laugh.

To the right, there is another door, this one to the outside. People escape from the door for a nervous cigarette or bathroom visit. I won't be using it. The walls are painted black. A red light provides a little light without interfering with anything on stage. Opposite the outside door are the stairs down to the dressing room. They are bumpy and uneven, worn due to almost a century of use. They are too dangerous for me to use. I will stay at the side of the stage, amongst the dusty black curtains and the stage ladders, listening to the audience's chatter as the other actors take up their opening positions onstage.

It is nice to be back.

A Grand Old Time

A cherished Blackpool oasis
An escape from any sadness
With performance at its basis
That sits alongside the madness.

Where for over a hundred years
Be it music, farce or drama,
Old troupers bowed to claps and cheers
Forgetting their real-life trauma.

It's crowded outside the stage door.
Everyone's waiting for the stars
Who appear to a great uproar
As they try to get to their cars.

Now that I am in a wheelchair
The stage door no more can beckon
Unfit to feel the footlights glare
Performer no more, they reckon.

Once, I was part of the magic
Though now I just sit there and watch.
Please don't think that I am tragic
I'll dial my resolve up a notch.

From performing, I won't abstain.
Although I cannot kick my heels
I will make it onstage again
I'll just simply do it on wheels.

15th August 1945 9.30 pm V.J. Night

Today is my 34th birthday and not one person has wished me "Many happy returns", but I know my little Biddy will have been thinking of me, even if we couldn't be together.

I had thought that there would be celebrations tonight, now that the war is finally over. We've all been away from our loved ones for far too long. Out in the desert for all those years and now stuck in this godforsaken hole. To think I thought the desert was bad.

I've missed my children growing up. I've not even met the youngest, my little Patricia. I know I shouldn't complain because I am going back to them, there are plenty that can't say that, I know that I'm one of the lucky ones. It's just that I don't feel all that lucky tonight. We should be celebrating, because we can. Yet we're not. I'm miserable and I shouldn't be. I feel guilty because I am. You don't complain and I haven't before. I'd never say it out loud but I think I deserve a moan as it's worse now it is over and yet I'm still not with my family. I'm back in this country and yet we are still far apart, so near and yet so far.

My little Biddy has kept it all going at home, she looks after everyone but herself. I know she goes hungry to stretch the rationing for the kiddies. That's just her. I'll never change her but I wish I could give her the world. Mind you, I've seen more of the world and I wouldn't give you tuppence for it. Once I get home I'm never going anywhere again. Bloody desert, the only sand I want to see from now on is on Blackpool beach, maybe Cleveleys for a day out, but that's it.

This place Gomer is the most miserable place in the world. People should be enjoying themselves tonight after waiting so long, but not in this joint. They're just boring and miserable. I wish I'd been at home with my love, we sure would have had a good time. In this place, they don't know what life is. I went out about 7:30 and I managed to get a couple of pints. But then I came back to my billet disgusted at their attitude.

I'm going to write to my little Biddy and hope and pray that we will be together again soon. I will sign off as always to her

"Love and God bless, fondest love and kisses from your ever-loving husband Bill."

Cowritten with my Grandad William Sandwell 1911-1966 from one of his last war letters to my Nan. If only he had known he would be home for good within the fortnight, and baby number four would be on his way.

All that glitters

When I was a girl, I was ashamed of my knickers. They were grey. They were meant to be white. They were clean, but they were a dirty shade of grey. I was embarrassed when it was PE. I was embarrassed to be poor. Now. I'm embarrassed by that. I'm ashamed. It's no sin to be poor, is it? I should have felt proud that Mam, a widow, was bringing up three little ones. She hadn't even had our Jane when Dad died; she was only three months along. I'm so ashamed that I didn't see all she did for us; all she provided. All I could see was the lack.

Mam understood, though; she was kind like that. She used to call me her little magpie. If we ever had a sweet, I'd save the shiny paper. I'd polish our cheap knives and forks till they sparkled. I begged her to take the pretty buttons off my cardigan before she passed it down to our Jane. I loved those buttons, you see. If you held them up to the light, they glittered and sparkled.

I love glitter. I love sparkles. I love pretty things. No, I don't need to be analysed to work out why I love glitter; I know it's because of those damn grey knickers. I love pretty things because I never had them when I was a child.

I've got them now, though. Oh, I know people laugh at me because I wear too much jewellery, too much makeup. I like to be overdressed.

"Oh, Karen, you always look like you're going to a wedding." says my neighbour, Mrs Langley. She couldn't say anything better to me.

I don't really do casual. I do have jeans, but they're studded with rhinestones. I do have flat sandals, but they're completely encrusted with sequins. I love sequins. I love glitter. My nephew calls me Aunty Sequins; he's my favourite.

I'd have everything sparkling if I could. I might be getting older, and I might need varifocals, but they come out of the glittery case.

I've recently discovered this rhinestone ribbon roll in The Range. I love The Range. They have lots of glittery things in there. Mirrors, towels, wallpaper, and even glittery paint. Paint with glitter in! I've got that in every room. But this ribbon is only cheap; you can glue it on everything and I have. My tissue box holder is sparkly, the surround of my television is sparkly and even the toilet brush is sparkly. It's the best thing I've found.

I sit on the couch at night (I've covered the wooden feet with the rhinestone ribbon – it looks fab-u-lous!). I settle down to watch my favourite TV programme. I look around and everything glitters, everything sparkles and it's all so pretty.

Anyway, must go Strictly is starting now. That's a programme that knows all about sparkle.

Advice Inc.

Always remember your truth,

Is the only story to tell.

Always remember your worth,

Is not measured in pounds and pence.

Always remember your help,

Is more important than you know.

Always remember your fight,

Is sometimes just walking away.

Always remember your strength,

Is simply being true to you.

Always remember your best

Is all that anyone can ask.

Always remember your love,

Is what people will remember.

Interior Design

Him:

How dare you! This was all your idea – I didn't want to do it anyway.

Her:

I didn't think it would look like this, though.

Him:

I tried to tell you, but you stopped listening because you wanted your way as usual. I knew this room was too cold to be painted blue. It's north facing, I did tell you.

Her:

I didn't think it would be like standing in a fridge. I just wanted a change, something different.

Him:

Well, you get your wish. It's certainly different. Why this shade? What's it called, invalid car blue?"

Her:

I had it especially mixed. I took that little Buddha statue from the garden and they scanned it. It's such a lovely shade out there in the sunshine.

Him:

Well, it's not lovely in here. How much did that cost, specially mixed paint?

Her:

No more than that antique bookend you bought last week at the antiques fair. A complete waste of money. What's the use of one book end? It's like a gun without a trigger.

Him:

Be grateful that we haven't got a gun with a trigger. This room is making me feel suicidal.

Her:

Oh, take a chill pill, you drama queen. It's only paint. Come on; we'll go to B and Q and get something bright and sunny. Yellow, I think.

Him:

That will feel like I'm sitting in a big tub of Utterly Butterly.

Her:

What do you suggest, then?

Him:

Magnolia, plain old magnolia.

Her:

It will look like an institution, a prison cell.

Him:

Well, don't call it magnolia, then call it 'white chocolate' like Laurence Llewelyn-Bowen did. Give it some attitude.

Her:

Come on then, Tiger, magnolia it is. I'm having magenta cushions and a fuchsia rug, then.

Him:

Oh, God.

Our 'enry

So, where did my little lad go?
Wasn't it a moment ago
He was trying to tie his laces.
Now he has hair in strange places.
Once tucked in bed by half past six.
Now up all night to get his kicks.

He listened to stories on my knee
And how he can grow a goatee.
He held my hand so tightly then,
Those days won't come around again.
Hours I spent by the football field
Waiting for his keenness to yield.
I still don't know the offside rule,
But I tried not to look like a fool.
I'm proud to say I tried my best.
Smiled and looked suitably impressed.
Then came the running; that was fine
As he crossed the finishing line.
Now he's a fledgling dancing star.
Those who know, say he could go far.
A charmer with a cheeky wit,
He'll sweet talk you and just won't quit.
Now with letters after his name,
First-class degree to much acclaim.
Onstage in his gown, looking slick
And we always thought he was thick.

ON BROADWAY

"They say the neon lights are bright on Broadway. They say there's always magic in the air."

(On Broadway, written by Mike Stoller · Barry Mann · Cynthia Weil, · Jerry Leiber).

Well, I grew up looking at the neon lights of Broadway. No, not the one in New York. The neon lights of the Broadway of my childhood were on the paper shop opposite my house in Fleetwood, Lancashire.

I never realised what a strange position we lived in. From the front door, you could see a paper shop, an Open All Hours shop, Chinese takeaway, a chemist, undertakers, a pub, Ford Garage, a petrol station, a taxi rank, a bus stop, a telephone box, an Old people's home and a doctors surgery. It was also three doors up from possibly the busiest roundabout in any residential area. With eight exits. Yes, eight. When friends from out of town visited me when I was older, they marvelled at my calmness as I navigated this roundabout. I allowed them to be impressed until I reminded them that every journey I had ever made since I was a small child involved this roundabout. Every driving lesson involved this roundabout; it was my norm.

We lived in a bungalow bought from my godparents. So, although it wasn't my first home, it was a home I've always known. My godparents had put an upstairs in the loft. So, we found ourselves a young family surrounded by retired folk. It was the ideal position for the retired because they never had to travel anywhere if they didn't want to. Everything they needed was at hand. Even the undertakers were just across the road. My parents still live there, almost 50 years now. They have a funeral plan with the undertakers. Mum is livid as she thinks the fee for transporting to the undertakers should be reduced. They do live in sight of it, after all.

"Private ambulance," she said. "We've got a perfectly good wheelbarrow in the garage. Use that."

I am grateful every day that we haven't reached that point yet.

The doctor's surgery was another converted bungalow next door but one. It was not our surgery; we had to travel into town. My Nan loved Thursdays best; she positioned herself in front of the huge window, adjusted the vertical blinds and settled down to watch Pregnancy Thursday. She took great pleasure in watching the ladies of the town blossom. She was quite happy to miss Thursday's episode of Take the High Road or The Young Doctors. This was much more interesting.

Occasionally people mistook our bungalow for the doctor's surgery. I'm unsure how they did this because our bungalow had a garden in front, not a car park. An unfortunate design fault of our bungalow was that the toilet was opposite the front door. Imagine my surprise emerging from the toilet as a naked 19-year-old about to take a shower when I found a somewhat confused old lady standing in the middle of the hallway. She was shocked, as she's only popped in for her prescription. We both screamed until she realised there was no reception desk and she was trespassing. I thought she lingered a bit too long afterwards. My Dad found it all rather amusing when he got home from his shift and muttered something about "widow's memories."

When I moved back home after university, my childhood doctor refused to take me back on their books, so I ended up at the doctor's surgery next door but one. It was there, with my trousers round my ankles, having a rather intimate examination, that I watched my mum peg out the washing in our garden; it was a little surreal.

Next door to the left was Mr and Mrs Cooper. Maggie was kind. She died suddenly on a Sunday morning in 1978. She was a big spiritualist, and they put a plaque up to her memory in the spiritualist church. Above it was a shelf with an eternal flame always switched on. In fact, it was a bedside light with a twisty pink plastic shade. I had all the rehearsals for my childhood shows in that church. I spent far too long worrying about what would happen if the power went out, a fuse blew, or the bulb broke. I worried far too much about the eternal nature of Maggie's flame. I'm worrying about it now. I think I better move on.

Mr Cooper remarried quickly, the new Mrs Cooper was friendly too. She had a tan, big earrings, lots of pink lipstick and a Datsun Cherry. They moved to Ibiza. We called into their apartment when we were on holiday. They were thrilled to see us; I think they were a little bit bored.

To the right, initially was an old couple with a bubble car. It rarely came out of the garage, but when it did, the whole house shook. I love that little Heinkel. I still want a car with a window and bonnet as a door. I just do.

Across the road was the paper shop. It eventually expanded into a Mini Mart. I was sad about this. I missed it being a paper shop with a proper counter with sweets on shelves behind. I missed the chemist when it went too. It was a real chemist with the smell of camphor and menthol. It was a chemist that never tried to be anything other than what it was. There were no sweets or anything like that, just a rack of barley sugar lollies on the counter, and these were only kept in case a diabetic had a funny turn whilst in the queue. The chemist had grumpy assistants wearing Dr Scholl sandals. I think they tried to cheer themselves up by trying out all the various perms and hair dyes using their staff discount. They never cheered up despite ever-changing hair colours by Nice and Easy and some truly remarkable wash-and-wear 'Twink' perms. I loved the beautiful glass bottles in the window. I missed those bottles when the undertakers eventually knocked through into the chemists. I presume they told the chemist first.

The Chinese takeaway might have been convenient, but we didn't use it. My mom preferred to jump into the Vauxhall Nova and pop into town after the baby rabbit incident. My friend and I caught a baby rabbit (kitten, I used to be a teacher) escaping from the yard of the Chinese. It transpired that they were breeding them to pass off as chicken. My friend nursed the rabbit, but it didn't survive. The Chinese is still there, probably 20 owners along by now, but my mum will still only pop over for rice or chips and she's never had chicken and cashew nuts again.

The pub is gone too now. I went in there, although I didn't drink until I met my wife. Being a teetotal vegetarian was too much like hard work for her, so within a fortnight of us dating, I was drunk with a bacon sandwich in my hand. The pub was a known haven for underage drinkers. When the landlord rang the bell for the last orders, he always used to add,

"Let's have you. You've all got school in the morning."

The pub installed a bungee jump in the car park one weekend. It was a new thing. What a weekend that was. We could stand in the porch to watch and listen to the screams. My Nan couldn't stand in the porch by that time, so Mum put a deck chair out front for her. She loved it. She thought they were mad and screamed along with them. She also asked for her tea outside on a tray on her knee; bless her.

By this time, we had Mrs Hatch next door to us on the left. She was lovely, a Fleetwood lass who had married a Welsh gentleman farmer and moved away. When widowed she had returned. She settled down next to us to see out her days with daily visits from her sister, who lived around the corner. She appeared in charity shows at the local Old People's Hall. It turns out that she could be a saucy little minx when she thought she could get the audience laughing. She wasn't above raising her skirt to show her bloomers if she felt it was needed to get a laugh. I thought she was marvellous.

So that only leaves 'across the back', that's the bungalow round the corner. When I was a small boy, the lady who lived there shouted at me as I peeked over the fence at her poodle. That's not a euphemism. It was a little grey poodle. It had one eye and I loved it. I always have a poodle of my own to love nowadays, though it's hard to find a grey one with one eye. I never forgot that telling off or her wrath when the pegs holding my swing came loose in the wet grass. This sent both me and my swing flying backwards into the shared fence. It was hardly my fault, was it? One minute I was flying high on my swing and then the next minute, I was actually flying. She moved after that. A couple of other people moved in over the decades. After 40 years, she was back. It turns out that she'd always owned the bungalow and had rented it out. She smiled at me over the fence not so long ago, I nearly told her to keep her eyes off my poodle, but I resisted the temptation.

Printed in Great Britain
by Amazon